The Messy First Christmas

The Messy Lives Surrounding the Birth of Jesus
Floyd Gary Pierce

Discipleship Studio

To my parents, Gary Pierce and Anita Williams.
Thank you for all my Christmas memories.

The Messy First Christmas
The Messy Lives Surrounding the Birth of Jesus

Paperback ISBN: 978-1-965044-05-6

Requests for information should be addressed to:
Discipleship Studio, 186 Woodbrier Dr, Scottsville, Kentucky 42164

Scripture quotations are from The ESV® Bible (The Holy Bible,
English Standard Version®), copyright © 2001 by Crossway, a
publishing ministry of Good News Publishers. Used by permission. All
rights reserved.

Contents

Introduction

If you're reading this book, Christmas is probably getting close. Anticipation grows as Christmas Day approaches. Your world changes from its normal routine. It's busier, yet slower. Days are fuller. If your home is like mine, the countdown to December 25 is on display. Meaningful traditions from the past are now more significant than a month ago. You find yourself more sentimental, kinder, patient, and perhaps more charitable. Christmas is the most wonderful time of the year, isn't it?

Christmas won't happen unless you tackle your exploding to-do list. Your shopping list is growing. The decorations need displaying. You must plan meals and coordinate with the extended family. Parties fill your calendar. School and church obligations grow. It's feeling like Christmas.

For some, Christmas brings happy memories of family. For others, it is a reminder of loneliness. From pain and heartache to sweet memories of togetherness, Christmas magnifies the emotions we store up throughout the year. Nothing is normal right now, and that somehow feels normal.

Christmas is different now. From your childhood memories to today, it's not the same. Christmas today looks very different from the first Christmas. So much of our modern Christmas is absent from the Biblical account of the birth of our Savior, Jesus.

Christmas today is commercial. It brings retailers into profit for the year. The first Christmas reveals hope hidden by the world today. It began in the normal routine of life. The first Christmas became anything but normal. A silent night brought hope and purpose.

You might give anything for a silent night this Christmas season. Thoughts of your extended family invading your home may give you anxious thoughts. The endless chores that no one around you is helping with may overwhelm you. You probably think to yourself, "Why do we do this every year?" Christmas is chaotic.

Thank you for picking up this little book during your busiest season of the year. Whether you are seeking a brief escape from the chaos or looking to grow in your understanding of the first Christmas, I trust this book will help you see that the extended family around Jesus wasn't perfect, either. In fact, it was messy, very messy. It's through this messiness that beauty comes. Our Savior, Jesus, came into His Creation messy. He understands the chaos that surrounds you, and that brings comfort and joy. There is hope that God sees you in the middle of this mess and He shows you He understands. God understands. He is with you. Immanuel means "God with us."

Merry Christmas!

Floyd Gary Pierce

Chapter One

Zechariah and Elizabeth

In the days of Herod, king of Judea, there was a priest named Zechariah, of the division of Abijah. And he had a wife from the daughters of Aaron, and her name was Elizabeth. And they were both righteous before God, walking blamelessly in all the commandments and statutes of the Lord. But they had no child, because Elizabeth was barren, and both were advanced in years. (Luke 1:5-7 [English Standard Version]).

Righteous, Blameless, and Barren

From the outside looking in, you would think a priest and his wife might have it all together. Zechariah and Elizabeth lived a life full of devotion to God and to the commandments. The gospel writer, Luke, tells us they were righteous and blameless. This is important for a Jewish priest. Zechariah would have to stand between God and the people, and he better be righteous.

They might have had it all together on the outside, but if you have ever longed for a child and struggled with infertility, then you know they were probably a mess on the inside.

Zechariah and Elizabeth were both of priestly descent, in the line of Aaron. They were older and barren, even though they were righteous and blameless. Since they were older, they had really given up hope of having a child of their own. While our modern culture may not stigmatize childlessness, the first century Jewish culture did. In their culture, it was a sign of misfortune for the barren couple. Even though modern culture may not stigmatize childlessness, for many who are childless, there is an internal desire for children. Their absence creates a void that feels like misfortune.

Zechariah and Elizabeth must have felt that void in their lives and the stigma that their culture placed on them. It must have hurt.

Now while he was serving as priest
before God when his division was on

duty, according to the custom of the priesthood, he was chosen by lot to enter the temple of the Lord and burn incense. And the whole multitude of the people were praying outside at the hour of incense. And there appeared to him an angel of the Lord standing on the right side of the altar of incense. And Zechariah was troubled when he saw him, and fear fell upon him. (Luke 1:8-12.)

Not Your Typical Day at the Office

Have you ever seen an angel? Yeah, me neither. At least, I don't think so. Have you ever noticed that when angels show up in the Bible, they cause people to be overcome with fear? Apparently, angels are not cute little chubby babies with wings riding on clouds. Angels cause fear. Fear overtakes Zechariah right as he is about to do a once in a lifetime thing. He was going to enter the temple and burn incense.

You may think he's a priest. That's what priests do, right? Yes, but there are a lot of priests in Israel. There were 24 priestly orders. This means that each order would serve in the temple for two weeks out of the year. During that time period, they chose Zechariah from his order to enter the temple and burn incense. This is a high privilege that only comes around once in a lifetime.

I am not sure how this all played out, but I imagine Zechariah is a little nervous and a lot excited about getting to enter the temple and do his priestly duty. He knows no one will come in after him. Zechariah goes in alone. He is in there and then this angel shows up with an unbelievable message.

> But the angel said to him, "Do not be afraid, Zechariah, for your prayer has been heard, and your wife Elizabeth will bear you a son, and you shall call his name John. And you will have joy and gladness, and many will rejoice at his birth, for he will be great before the Lord. And he must not drink wine or strong drink, and he will be filled with the Holy Spirit, even from his mother's womb. (Luke 1:13-15.)

When Life Seemed Hopeless, God Revealed He Had Different Plans

Zechariah and Elizabeth were hopeless. Their advanced years and history of barrenness left little reason to think there would be a baby's cry in their home. Though they were hopeless, they had faithfully prayed for a child. They appealed to God to give them a child. In their hopelessness, they held onto hope somehow. The angel shows up unexpectedly and has an unbelievable message. That's the other thing about angels in the Bible; their messages are unbelievable.

God uses this moment in Zechariah's life to let him know He has different plans. Change was coming. Life has been going one way for Zechariah and his wife. Pain and disappointment marked Zechariah and his wife's life together, despite their lives of obedience and faithfulness towards God. They would soon welcome a baby to their home. One that would bring joy to many. One that is special. One that will be filled with the Holy Spirit. Zechariah and Elizabeth were about to have a miracle child.

Miracle Baby with a Mission

"And he will turn many of the children of Israel to the Lord their God, and he will go before him in the spirit and power of Elijah, to turn the hearts of the fathers to the children, and the disobedient to the wisdom of the just, to make ready for the Lord a people prepared." (Luke 1:16-17.)

This miracle baby will do some amazing things to prepare the way for the Christmas miracle baby to come. Let's take a quick look at what this baby was going to do. First, "he will turn many of the children of Israel to the Lord their God." This must mean that many of the children of Israel had turned away from the Lord their God.

Look at the last paragraph of the Old Testament.

> "Behold, I will send you Elijah the prophet before the great and awesome day of the LORD comes. And he will turn the hearts of fathers to their children and the hearts of children to their fathers, lest I come and strike the land with a decree of utter destruction." (Malachi 4:5-6.)

These were the last words spoken by God to close out the Old Testament. Then silence. Four hundred years of silence. The last thing Malachi prophesied is that someone is coming. Hold on to hope. Someone is coming. Someone is coming, then someone even greater is coming. John, later to be known as the

Baptist, is this miracle baby to point the way to the LORD. This is amazing news. Four hundred years of silence is about to be broken.

This miracle child will point people back to the LORD. The Old Testament is full of stories of the people of Israel turning away from the LORD. God would show grace and then they would return, but only for a little while. There are four hundred years of silence from the LORD. God has been quiet. Four hundred years may not seem like too many years considering we are two thousand years from this first Christmas, but generations have come and gone during this silence and there must be many people in Israel who have turned their back to the LORD.

Doubt It

> And Zechariah said to the angel, "How shall I know this? For I am an old man, and my wife is advanced in years." (Luke 1:18.)

Zechariah doubted this good news. He did the math. He counted up their years, and he knew what the angel was saying was impossible. Remember, Zechariah was a priest. He was a professional believer. His response was doubt, not unbelief. Perhaps all the years of being childless had broken his heart too much. He remained painfully doubtful, even though there was an angel right in front of him telling him what God was about to do.

Zechariah should have known that God can do impossible things. In his pain, he simply rejected God's ability or willingness to do impossible things for him. God has done impossible things in the past. Zechariah knew, studied, and believed the Old Testament, the Hebrew Bible. Surely, he would have recognized God's ability to do impossible things in the stories of Abraham and Sarah. Surely, Zechariah would have recognized this pattern in others, too.

But no, the message was too great. His pain was too much. Zechariah doubted. It was impossible for him. Even though Zechariah was performing the highest honor of his profession. In that moment, his faith was weak. He couldn't believe the message of the angel.

Can you imagine being in the temple, the holiest of places, encountering an angel with a message you have longed to hear your entire lifetime, receiving a positive answer to a prayer request that you and your spouse have prayed for for many years, and not having the faith to believe it?

What does that say about this priest, Zechariah?

This narrative shows you he is not much different from you. God is at work in your life, but faith is often weakest when you need it the most.

Have you recognized this in your life? Faith is often weakest when you need it the most. It's hard to believe good news when you are used to living through only bad news. Have you ever doubted God because your pain is just too much?

It's hard to believe that God is at work when you haven't seen His work in your life. It's hard to hear from God when He has been silent for four hundred years. It's hard to believe in miracles when you only look at the facts as you see them.

Zechariah isn't much different from you, is he?

Doubt Has Consequences

And the angel answered him, "I am Gabriel. I stand in the presence of God, and I was sent to speak to you and to bring you this good news. And behold, you will be silent and unable to speak until the day that these things take place, because you did not believe my words, which will be fulfilled in their time." And the people were waiting for

Zechariah, and they were wondering at
his delay in the temple. And when he
came out, he was unable to speak to
them, and they realized that he had
seen a vision in the temple. And he kept
making signs to them and remained
mute. And when his time of service was
ended, he went to his home. (Luke
1:19-23.)

Put yourself in Gabriel's shoes for a moment.
Gabriel is an angel. He is a messenger. He has had
a front-row seat to God's faithfulness for countless
years, possibly since Creation. Gabriel knows God
to be faithful and Gabriel has been on the delivering
side of God's promises in the past.

It's unclear what all Gabriel knows in this moment,
but he surely knows something big is getting ready
to happen. He is only called in when big things
are about to happen. I assume Gabriel is excited
to witness God once again proving Himself to the
world, and then Gabriel faces this doubting priest.

Gabriel hears the objections from Zechariah.
Gabriel listens, then speaks. When Gabriel speaks,
he goes from being a messenger to becoming a
prophet for just a moment. Perhaps Gabriel is
remembering God speaking to Job, saying "Where
were you when ..." (Job 38:4-7.) In the Job account,

Job promises to be silent after he speaks his mind to the LORD. Here Gabriel silences Zechariah for his doubt. The more I study and consider Gabriel here, the more I really like him. This might be some of his finest work as an angel.

Faith You Can Feel

> After these days his wife Elizabeth conceived, and for five months she kept herself hidden, saying, "Thus the Lord has done for me in the days when he looked on me, to take away my reproach among people." (Luke 1:24-25.)

One day, your faith will become sight. You will go from believing to seeing. Elizabeth responded better than her husband to this impossible news, but maybe she was prepared for this moment. She could feel the pregnancy. Even if it was too difficult to believe, she felt it. But you wonder if she worried it might not fully take. She kept herself hidden. Perhaps in her pain, she had a lingering doubt that even though she felt the little one inside her, the pregnancy wouldn't last.

Elizabeth makes a beautiful, faith-filled statement in verse 25. She gave credit to the LORD. She recognized that biologically, it was impossible. Even theoretically, it was impossible. But with God, it was possible. Elizabeth held on to hope.

If the Christmas season is anything, it is a season of hope. Elizabeth is the first one to see that. She doesn't know what's about to unfold in the greater story of her extended family, but for her immediate family, hope sets in.

Let's continue looking at Elizabeth. Let's look at her visit with her cousin, Mary. Before you read about their visit, I will let you know that Gabriel, the same angel who visited Zechariah, visits Mary and gives her similar news. It's even more impossible, but we will save that story for a later chapter. Just know Mary is with child. Let's read about their visit in Luke 1:35-45.

Mary and Elizabeth

And the angel answered her (Mary), "The Holy Spirit will come upon you, and the power of the Most High will overshadow you; therefore the child to be born will be called holy—the Son of God. And behold, your relative Elizabeth in her old age has also conceived a son, and this is the sixth month with her who was called barren. For nothing will be impossible with God." And Mary said, "Behold, I am the servant of the Lord; let it be to me according to your word." And the angel departed from her.

In those days, Mary arose and went with haste into the hill country, to a town in Judah, and she entered the house of Zechariah and greeted Elizabeth. And when Elizabeth heard the greeting of Mary, the baby leaped in her womb. And Elizabeth was filled with the Holy Spirit, and she exclaimed with a loud cry, "Blessed are you among women, and blessed is the fruit of your womb! And why is this granted to me that the mother of my Lord should come to me? For behold, when the sound of your greeting came to my ears, the baby in my womb leaped for joy. And blessed is she who believed that there would be a fulfillment of what was spoken to her from the Lord." (Luke 1:35-45.)

Mary, a virgin, gets impossible news; she will conceive and bear a son.

Impossible.

Mary is told that her relative, Elizabeth, will also conceive and bear a son, even in her old age.

Impossible.

Perhaps all this great news is adding up in Gabriel's mind. Maybe he has seen the reaction of Zechariah and heard Mary's question, "How will this be?" Because Gabriel doesn't wait for doubt to be expressed. Gabriel says an accurate statement about God, "For nothing will be impossible with God."

For Nothing Will Be Impossible With God

Let's unpack that statement for just a moment. It is tempting to take this sentence and misapply it to many scenarios that it doesn't speak to. This sentence alone, taken out of context, can lead some to believe incorrect things about God. There are, in fact, many things that are not possible with or for God. It is impossible for God to cause you to sin. It is impossible for God to act outside of His revealed character. God cannot create a box so big that the box can contain Him.

So, if there are things that are impossible with God, what does Gabriel mean when he says this statement? Every misquoted Bible verse (there are many) has a context. The context will help you understand what is intended. Gabriel is saying that if God promises something, He will make it happen, even if it seems impossible. This is a correct statement. This is what the Bible is teaching. This is what Elizabeth, Mary, and Zechariah are living out. If God promises something, nothing is impossible with God.

What God wants to make happen, God will make happen.

Even if it seems impossible to us, nothing will be impossible with God. This is true for Zechariah and Elizabeth, and it is true for you and your family. What may seem impossible for you and your family is possible with God, if He has promised it in the Bible.

Remember, life for Zechariah and Elizabeth hadn't gone the way they had hoped. God didn't give them this child because they wanted him. God gave them this child because God was going to use this child to prepare the way for Jesus.

God's plans are better than your plans.

As you follow Jesus, remember that, especially if life isn't going the way you thought it would, trust that God is at work in your life even when you don't see it or understand it. God will accomplish what He wants. He is the main character in the unfolding story around you. His plans are better.

Sometimes, this is a hard message to hear. Especially if you are walking through pain and disappointment.

Trust that God is at work.

He may not give you exactly what you are looking for, but you can know that what He has for you is far better. What God has for you is for your good and His glory.

God will accomplish what He wants because nothing is impossible for God. Let's continue in Luke 1:57-66.

The Birth of a Miracle Child

> Now the time came for Elizabeth to give birth, and she bore a son. And her neighbors and relatives heard that the Lord had shown great mercy to her, and they rejoiced with her. And on the eighth day they came to circumcise the child. And they would have called him Zechariah after his father, but his mother answered, "No; he shall be

called John." And they said to her,
"None of your relatives is called by
this name." And they made signs to
his father, inquiring what he wanted
him to be called. And he asked for a
writing tablet and wrote, "His name
is John." And they all wondered. And
immediately his mouth was opened
and his tongue loosed, and he spoke,
blessing God. And fear came on all their
neighbors. And all these things were
talked about through all the hill country
of Judea and all who heard them laid
them up in their hearts, saying, "What
then will this child be?" For the hand of
the Lord was with him. (Luke 1:57-66.)

An impossible promise has been fulfilled. God once again proves His faithfulness to His Word. Elizabeth gives birth to a baby boy. Normally, they would name the son after his father. But remember, Gabriel said to Zechariah, they were to name him John. Zechariah must have written that down throughout the pregnancy because he still could not speak. He was still suffering from the consequences of his doubt.

This miracle child, John, would grow up to be Jesus' weird cousin. You can read about John the Baptist in Matthew 3 to really understand what makes him the weird cousin.

When baby John is born, they circumcise him and announce his name. It is then that Zechariah can speak. What does he say? For months, Zechariah could not speak. He has expressed himself through writing, but he could not speak until now. When he speaks, what does he say? Let's look at the next part of this passage, Luke 1:67-79.

Zechariah Speaks

And his father Zechariah was filled with
the Holy Spirit and prophesied, saying,
"Blessed be the Lord God of Israel, for
he has visited and redeemed his people
and has raised up a horn of salvation
for us in the house of his servant David,
as he spoke by the mouth of his holy
prophets from of old, that we should be
saved from our enemies and from the
hand of all who hate us; to show the
mercy promised to our fathers and to
remember his holy covenant, the oath
that he swore to our father Abraham,
to grant us that we, being delivered
from the hand of our enemies, might

serve him without fear, in holiness
and righteousness before him all our
days. And you, child, will be called the
prophet of the Most High; for you will
go before the Lord to prepare his ways,
to give knowledge of salvation to his
people in the forgiveness of their sins,
because of the tender mercy of our God,
whereby the sunrise shall visit us from
on high to give light to those who sit
in darkness and in the shadow of death,
to guide our feet into the way of peace."
(Luke 1:67-79.)

This is a praise and a prophecy. People often refer
to this passage as the Benedictus.

The first thing Zechariah does when he can speak
is he praises God. He has had to sit quietly for
about nine months. The last words he spoke were
of doubting God's plans and power.

This doubting priest turned into a prophet. Silence
can clarify our thinking. Silence can help us hear
from God in His Word. Silence surely clarified things
for Zechariah, because the next things he spoke
were the foundations of the gospel message.

He praised the God he doubted. He then made
connections between the ideas presented in the Old

Testament. The hope that he had given up on was now overflowing out of his heart and mind through his words. Zechariah went from hopeless to hopeful.

This Christmas season, maybe that is where you are, hopeless.

If we are honest with each other, we have all gone through seasons of hopelessness. Don't be discouraged if that is the season you find yourself in this Christmas season. In your hopelessness, keep seeking God's plan.

It might take some silence and some time to sort through. In your hopelessness, know that God is faithful. Spend time in His Word. Look for God, even if you already know Him, and especially if you don't. Look for God this Christmas season and perhaps make this the season you praise the God you once doubted.

Chapter Two

Joseph

Now the birth of Jesus Christ took place
in this way. When his mother Mary
had been betrothed to Joseph, before
they came together she was found to
be with child from the Holy Spirit. And
her husband Joseph, being a just man
and unwilling to put her to shame,
resolved to divorce her quietly. But as
he considered these things, behold, an
angel of the Lord appeared to him in
a dream, saying, "Joseph, son of David,
do not fear to take Mary as your wife,
for that which is conceived in her is
from the Holy Spirit. She will bear a son,
and you shall call his name Jesus, for he
will save his people from their sins." All
this took place to fulfill what the Lord
had spoken by the prophet: "Behold, the
virgin shall conceive and bear a son,

and they shall call his name
Immanuel"
  (which means, God with us).

When Joseph woke from sleep, he did as
the angel of the Lord commanded him:
he took his wife, but knew her not until
she had given birth to a son. And he
called his name Jesus. (Matthew 1:18-25.)

A Carpenter Faced with a Difficult and Heartbreaking Decision

Joseph found himself in a surprising mess. Joseph was a carpenter. Being a carpenter, he probably crafted furniture because, at that time, houses were built with stone.

Have you ever considered how old Joseph was when Jesus was born? Or are you like me and just assumed he must of have been young because we know Mary to be a teenager? If you are around any Roman Catholic family members this Christmas season, ask them how old Joseph was when Jesus was born. Their answer may surprise you.

The Bible doesn't give us any sign of how old Joseph was. If the Bible is silent on this, it must not be important for our faith. So we should

say with certainty that we don't know how old
Joseph was when Jesus was born. But because
the Roman Catholic Church regards some of their
other writings as equal to, if not more important to
Scripture, let's consider the age of Joseph briefly.
Your Catholic friends and family will probably tell
you that Joseph could have been in his middle 50s
when Jesus was born. 5-0. Fifty. That seems odd,
doesn't it? It's old for a teenage spouse. Some may
say 30s, maybe even as young as late 20s.

The Roman Catholic Church has to maintain that
Joseph was much older than Mary, because the
Bible tells us that Jesus had siblings. He had at
least four brothers and several sisters. The Roman
Catholic Church maintains Mary remained a virgin
her entire life, so any siblings of Jesus must have had
to come from Joseph and his biblically unmentioned
previous marriage. Protestants assume Joseph was
older, but not that much older. The Bible says
nothing about Mary remaining a virgin, so we
shouldn't assume Mary was a virgin for her entire
life. We can presume Joseph to be closer to Mary's
age.

Joseph was probably in his late teens, 18 or
19. Just as there were stigmas associated with
barren couples in the Jewish culture we learned
about last week, there were stigmas associated
with unmarried people who were older than 20.

The Bible records nothing about a stigma with Joseph. Plus, in the Jewish culture, parents arrange marriages. This betrothal between Mary and Joseph would have been setup by their parents, or at least Mary's parents. Here is something from the Bible Knowledge Commentary regarding the marriage traditions of the day.

> Marriages were arranged for individuals by parents, and contracts were negotiated. After this was accomplished, the individuals were considered married and were called husband and wife. They did not, however, begin to live together. Instead, the woman continued to live with her parents and the man with his for one year. The waiting period was to demonstrate the faithfulness of the pledge of purity given concerning the bride. If she was found to be with child in this period, she obviously was not pure, but had been involved in an unfaithful sexual relationship. Therefore the marriage could be annulled. If, however, the one-year waiting period demonstrated the purity of the bride, the husband would

then go to the house of the bride's
parents and in a grand processional
march lead his bride back to his
home. There they would begin to live
together as husband and wife and
consummate their marriage physically.
Matthew's story should be read with
this background in mind.[1]

This is the setting of Mary and Joseph before the
birth of Jesus. They are in this one-year waiting
period to show the faithfulness of the Mary's purity.
It's important that we read the Bible understanding
the context of the Bible. They lived in a different
time, place, and culture than you live in today. This
waiting period is probably a foreign concept for you,
but as a father of two teenage daughters, I am really
beginning to like the concept of arranged marriages
more and more.

Now the birth of Jesus Christ took place
in this way. When his mother Mary had

---

1. Louis A. Barbieri Jr., "Matthew," in *The Bible
Knowledge Commentary: An Exposition of the
Scriptures*, ed. J. F. Walvoord and R. B. Zuck, vol.
2 (Wheaton, IL: Victor Books, 1985), 20.

been betrothed to Joseph, before they
came together she was found to be with
child from the Holy Spirit. (Matthew
1:18.)

Joseph and Mary are in this one-year waiting period
to make sure Mary is faithful to Joseph as her
parents arranged this marriage. The whole point
of this time was to wait and see if Mary would be
faithful, and then they found out she was pregnant.

Joseph must have been heartbroken and
embarrassed.

Can you imagine finding out that the one you
were going to marry was pregnant, and you knew
the baby wasn't yours? Even if it was an arranged
marriage, how would you feel? What would go
through your mind?

For most of us, our potential first responses to this
heartache and embarrassment might make for good
daytime television talk show material. We would
be absolutely heartbroken, deeply embarrassed,
painfully hurt, and perhaps we might start seeking
revenge. Our first thoughts would not be, this must
be something special. Our first thoughts would not
be Mary is innocent.

Honorable Response to Broken Promises

Joseph must have been heartbroken and embarrassed. Even though we read none of his thoughts in the Bible, we can plainly see his character. Joseph, in his pain and embarrassment, was a good man who must have loved Mary deeply. Let's look at his response in verse 19.

> And her husband Joseph, being a just
> man and unwilling to put her to
> shame, resolved to divorce her quietly.
> (Matthew 1:19.)

Finding out this terrible heartbreaking and embarrassing news, Joseph resolves to divorce her quietly. They aren't married yet, but because of their betrothal, a divorce is the only way to get out of this relationship alive.

Joseph took the high road when he could have taken Mary's life.

Joseph was a good man. The Bible says he was just and unwilling to put her to shame. He plans to divorce her quietly. Scripture gives Joseph the ability to be a just man and end this relationship differently. He could have had her stoned publicly. Let's look at the laws regarding a betrothed virgin who doesn't remain a virgin. Deuteronomy 22 says this:

> If there is a betrothed virgin, and a man
> meets her in the city and lies with her,
> then you shall bring them both out to
> the gate of that city, and you shall stone
> them to death with stones, the young
> woman because she did not cry for help
> though she was in the city, and the man
> because he violated his neighbor's wife.
> So you shall purge the evil from your
> midst. (Deuteronomy 22:23-24.)

This law from the Law of Moses gives us the consequences for a woman who is unfaithful during this betrothal time. This law assumes adultery because if it were rape, it assumes the virgin would cry out for help. If a betrothed woman is unfaithful, she was to be stoned to death, because adultery is evil. This isn't just the Jewish custom. Other cultures had similar practices, some included binding the adulterous couple and throwing them in water to drown them.

Look at the next few verses in Deuteronomy to see how the Law of Moses shows grace.

> But if in the open country a man meets
> a young woman who is betrothed, and

the man seizes her and lies with her,
then only the man who lay with her
shall die. But you shall do nothing to
the young woman; she has committed
no offense punishable by death. For this
case is like that of a man attacking
and murdering his neighbor, because
he met her in the open country, and
though the betrothed young woman
cried for help there was no one to
rescue her. (Deuteronomy 22:25-27.)

In cases of rape, grace is extended to the woman.
Deuteronomy shows the drama that is surrounding
the mother and earthly father of Jesus right before
he is born.

Christmas is Surrounded in Scandal

It is through this scandal that Jesus comes to
us. Perhaps it is helpful that there is scandal
surrounding His birth, because He would save us
from the scandals we so easily find ourselves in.
Jesus identifies with us in very real ways because
even though He is God, He became like us and
knows what it's like to be us.

Joseph could have ended it all from the very
beginning, but he didn't. He must have loved Mary

because he did not seek her stoning. He must have looked beyond his heartbreak and embarrassment and put Mary's life above his own reputation and future. Doesn't that reflect God's character and serve as an example for us?

God's love for you looks beyond the heartbreak that your sin causes Him in that He sent Jesus to take your punishment. The pain and embarrassment your sin must cause God is not counted against you when you love and follow Jesus, when you accept Jesus as your Lord.

What Joy There is in Christmas

What joy there is in Jesus!

Have you received Jesus as your Lord and Savior? This gift from God to overlook the pain and embarrassment your sin causes you and Him. This gift of Jesus, the very Son of God: have you committed your life to following Him? What grace there is for you when you do.

Joseph reflects God's character and love here for Mary. He gives you a worthy example worth following.

How quickly do you forgive someone when they cause you pain and embarrassment?

If you are like me, quick forgiveness often goes against your nature. Unconditional forgiveness is difficult, especially when the pain and embarrassment are great. But forgiveness is the call for the Christian.

Now, let me just say, I don't think we can know that Joseph has totally forgiven Mary yet. He has decided not to claim his rights and stone her to death, so there is grace and some forgiveness. However, he is looking to divorce her quietly; probably because the pain is just too great.

But then an angel shows up.

Remember from the last chapter. Angels show up and cause fear. They show up with a life-changing message and everything changes. Angels show up with a message from God.

Angels surround the story of the birth of Jesus. God is preparing the way for the birth of Jesus. Look at what the angel says in Matthew 1:20-23.

Then the Angel Shows Up

> But as he (Joseph) considered these things, behold, an angel of the Lord appeared to him in a dream, saying,

"Joseph, son of David, do not fear to
take Mary as your wife, for that which is
conceived in her is from the Holy Spirit.
She will bear a son, and you shall call his
name Jesus, for he will save his people
from their sins." All this took place to
fulfill what the Lord had spoken by the
prophet:

"Behold, the virgin shall conceive and
bear a son,
and they shall call his name Immanuel."
(Matthew 1:20-23.)

The angel shows up, causes fear, delivers a
life-changing message and changes everything.
This message from God comforts Joseph, heals his
heart, clears up any misunderstanding, and changes
everything.

Joseph encounters an angel who gives him hope and
comfort.

I think it is here we see Joseph completely turn back
toward Mary. We can't call it forgiveness because
nothing needs to be forgiven, but there is a total and
complete reconciliation. Joseph goes from desiring
to divorce her to bringing her into her home. Let's
look at the next two verses.

He Breaks Customs and Brings Her in to His Home

> When Joseph woke from sleep, he did
> as the angel of the Lord commanded
> him: he took his wife, but knew her
> not until she had given birth to a son.
> And he called his name Jesus. (Matthew
> 1:24-25.)

I don't think we fully realize what is happening here. Our cultural context doesn't pick up on Joseph's action. Let me bring out what is truly remarkable here.

I will quote from the Bible Knowledge Commentary again, because this commentator describes so well what you and I miss in just reading through these words.

> In light of this declaration Joseph was
> not to be afraid to take Mary into
> his home (Matt. 1:20). There would be
> misunderstanding in the community
> and much gossip at the well, but
> Joseph knew the true story of Mary's
> pregnancy and God's will for his life.

As soon as Joseph awakened from
this dream, he obeyed. He violated all
custom by immediately taking Mary
into his home rather than waiting till the
one-year time period of betrothal had
passed. Joseph was probably thinking
of what would be best for Mary in her
condition. He brought her home and
began to care and provide for her. [2]

Do you see the scandal? Notice the breaking of
custom? Do you see Joseph's love for Mary and
obedience to God?

This narrative goes from one scandalous event,
Mary's pregnancy during this one-year waiting
period, to the opposite scandal of Joseph breaking
the one-year waiting period and bringing her into
his home.

God is at work in life's messy situations. This
situation that Joseph and Mary find themselves in is
about as messy as one couple can be in, but we see
God is at work.

---

2. Louis A. Barbieri Jr., "Matthew," in *The Bible
Knowledge Commentary: An Exposition of the
Scriptures*, ed. J. F. Walvoord and R. B. Zuck, vol.
2 (Wheaton, IL: Victor Books, 1985), 20.

Look For God

Whatever messy situation you find yourself in this Christmas, look for God.

He is working.

God is there.

God is with you.

The angel quotes Isaiah and says they shall call his name Immanuel, which means God with us.

God is with you.

He is with you in the good and in the bad. He is with you when things are going well and He is with you when things are messy.

God is with you.

Why does it matter to know that God is with you? What changes in your life when you know God is there with you in the highest of moments and the lowest of moments? Why does it matter?

It should comfort you to know that the Maker of the universe is with you as you live your life in the world He created. But not only should you find comfort, you also have the power to walk through whatever lies ahead and hold on to God because He is with you. Strengthened in your spirit, you can obediently follow God and do the things He calls you to do, regardless of the consequences. Joseph gives you a great example worth following.

Joseph obediently follows God and brings Mary into his home. Joseph finds himself in a messy situation, one that he didn't sign up for and was getting ready to walk out of heartbroken. But God's plans are better. Joseph loved Mary, even when he thought she wasn't faithful. The message of the angel, a message of God's closeness, stopped Joseph and comforted and strengthened him. This is a wonderful love story, because as God comforted and strengthened Joseph in that vision while he slept, Joseph woke up with even more love for Mary.

Joseph goes and breaks the customs. This chapter started with it appearing that Mary sinfully broke the custom, but as God shows up in this messy situation, we see Mary was innocent and Joseph breaks the custom out of his great love for Mary and obedience to God.

This had to create gossip and rumors. Those things that were said behind their backs had to reach their ears and they probably were words that hurt. But Joseph remained faithful to Mary and to God.

Maybe you need God this Christmas. After the week you had, you realize you can't do this life without

Him. Don't let evil rob you of your hope. Don't let evil attempt to take away your trust.

Whatever messy situation you find yourself in this Christmas, look for God.

He is there and at work.

God is with you.

We shall call his name Immanuel, which means God with us.

God is with you.

> When I am afraid,
> I put my trust in you.
> In God, whose word I praise,
> in God I trust; I shall not be afraid.
> What can flesh do to me? (Psalm
> 56:3-4.)

Chapter Three

Mary

In the sixth month the angel Gabriel
was sent from God to a city of Galilee
named Nazareth, to a virgin betrothed
to a man whose name was Joseph, of the
house of David. And the virgin's name
was Mary. And he came to her and said,
"Greetings, O favored one, the Lord is
with you!" But she was greatly troubled
at the saying, and tried to discern what
sort of greeting this might be. And the
angel said to her, "Do not be afraid,
Mary, for you have found favor with
God. And behold, you will conceive in
your womb and bear a son, and you shall
call his name Jesus. He will be great and
will be called the Son of the Most High.
And the Lord God will give to him the
throne of his father David, and he will
reign over the house of Jacob forever,
and of his kingdom there will be no end."

And Mary said to the angel, "How will this be, since I am a virgin?"

And the angel answered her, "The Holy Spirit will come upon you, and the power of the Most High will overshadow you; therefore the child to be born will be called holy—the Son of God. And behold, your relative Elizabeth in her old age has also conceived a son, and this is the sixth month with her who was called barren. For nothing will be impossible with God." And Mary said, "Behold, I am the servant of the Lord; let it be to me according to your word." And the angel departed from her. (Luke 1:26-38.)

A Virgin Will Bear a Son, but First Some Background

The angel says some unbelievable things. This is nothing new for us, but it is new for Mary at this moment. She is betrothed to Joseph. Mary is a virgin. Yet, she will do the impossible. Mary will give birth to a son while being a virgin. This is an impossibly big deal. Why? Her son will be the Messiah.

The people of Israel had been waiting for the Messiah since almost the beginning of time. The first mention in the Bible of the need for a Messiah is back in the Garden of Eden, where God is speaking to the serpent.

> I will put enmity between you and the
> woman, and between your offspring
> and her offspring; he shall bruise your
> head, and you shall bruise his heel."
> (Genesis 3:15.)

This is right after the Fall. Sin entered God's perfect Creation at the Fall. Because of sin, there is a need for a Messiah, a Redeemer.   This was part of God's plan all along.

As time continued, sin continued.

The need for a Messiah became more and more visible. Here is what we see from the Prophet Isaiah concerning the Messiah and our sin.

> But he was pierced for our
> transgressions;

he was crushed for our iniquities;
upon him was the chastisement that
brought us peace,
and with his wounds we are healed.
All we like sheep have gone astray;
we have turned—every one—to
his own way;
and the LORD has laid on him
the iniquity of us all. (Isaiah 53:5-6.)

The Messiah would redeem the people who trust Him by being killed because of their sin. Verse six says that everyone sins. Everyone has turned away from God. The sin that began in Genesis with the Fall has reached each one of us. It has reached you. You need help to be made right with God. This is what the people of Israel had been waiting for thousands of years.

Mary Knew a Messiah Would Come

Mary knew a Messiah had to come. She, along with her family, her people, and, in fact, the entire world, needs the Messiah to come. That's where we pick up with Mary. This is where the angel shows up, causes fear, brings a life-changing message, and everything changes.

And the angel said to her, "Do not be afraid, Mary, for you have found favor with God. And behold, you will conceive in your womb and bear a son, and you shall call his name Jesus. He will be great and will be called the Son of the Most High. And the Lord God will give to him the throne of his father David, and he will reign over the house of Jacob forever, and of his kingdom there will be no end." (Luke 1:30-33, ESV.)

The angel shows up and says the Messiah is coming, and He is coming through Mary!

Mary Knew Confusion

Can you imagine this news?

The One you had been waiting for to make things right between God and man is coming. The One who was needed and prophesied for years would arrive in just nine months. The One who will redeem His people is coming through Mary. If you were Mary, how would you have responded?

Mary knew confusion because she knew herself. She knew biology. There was no way the Messiah could come through her. She voiced her confusion in verse 34.

> And Mary said to the angel, "How will
> this be, since I am a virgin?" (Luke 1:34,
> ESV.)

The angel explains to Mary that the Holy Spirit will come upon her and the Redeemer, the Messiah, the One who will make things right for those who follow Him will come through Mary because of the Holy Spirit. It's not because of biology.

In the first chapter, we looked at Mary's cousin, Elizabeth. She was also pregnant. Elizabeth was pregnant with Jesus' cousin, John the Baptist. In that chapter, I wrote, "What God wants to make happen, God will make happen."

This is true because verse 37 says,

> For nothing will be impossible with God.
> (Luke 1:37, ESV.)

What God wants to make happen, God will make happen.

Nothing is impossible with God. He created everything and sustains everything. God is sovereign, He is in control and rules over His Creation. He is all powerful. God is all knowing. He is in all places, at all times. God alone is God. Nothing will be impossible with God. What He wants to make happen, God will make happen. Mary knew this. Perhaps you need to be reminded of this at Christmas. What He wants to make happen, God will make happen. It is as true today as it was at the messy first Christmas.

Mary Knew God, and How to Trust Him

Mary followed God and knew of His faithfulness in the past. Mary knew that His faithfulness wouldn't stop. God is trustworthy. That is how, even in her confusion about the details, she could say this in verse 38.

> And Mary said, "Behold, I am the servant of the Lord; let it be to me according to your word." (Luke 1:38, ESV.)

Mary trusted God with a humanly speaking, impossible plan to bring forward the Messiah. This verse in Luke 1:38 is a tremendous verse for those of us who follow Jesus. Let this verse be true of you.

"I am the servant of the Lord; let it be to me according to your word."

What faith Mary must have in God with a statement like this. What trust she has in God.

Do you trust God in this way?

"Let it be to me according to your word."

If you are like me, sometimes we think we want God to honor our plans. We want to tell God how we think it should be and we want His blessing on our plans, but God's plans are much better than our plans. God is bigger and better than we can imagine. His plans for you are better. It's not always easy to see, but it is always true.

Mary accepted God's plan for her life and trusted God with it. It's this kind of trust, this is the faith that leads to real worship.

Mary Knew God, and How to Worship Him

Mary recognized God's plans were better, even if she didn't fully understand the details. She knew of God's faithfulness and she accepted these impossible plans as her reality and she worshipped God. Look at how she worships God in her song of praise, the Magnificat.

> And Mary said,
> "My soul magnifies the Lord,

and my spirit rejoices in God my Savior,
for he has looked on the humble estate
of his servant.
For behold, from now on all
generations will call me blessed;
for he who is mighty has done great
things for me,
and holy is his name.
And his mercy is for those who fear him
from generation to generation.
He has shown strength with his arm;
he has scattered the proud in the
thoughts of their hearts;
he has brought down the mighty from
their thrones
and exalted those of humble estate;
he has filled the hungry with good
things,
and the rich he has sent away empty.
He has helped his servant Israel,
in remembrance of his mercy,
as he spoke to our fathers,
to Abraham and to his offspring
forever." (Luke 1:46-55.)

Can I give you a little Christmas homework?

I would encourage you this Christmas season,
as your busy calendars slow up, in the last few

days of the year, to spend some time and write
out a praise to God. Use Mary's words as a
guide. Take some quiet alone time with a Bible and
your thoughts. Prayerfully consider what Christmas
means and how it has affected your life, and the life
of your family. Write some words down. If you can
do it poetically, wonderful. If you prefer a narrative
or story, that's great, too.

What has God brought you out of?

What has He rescued you from?

What promises from the Bible are you still holding
on to and trusting God to deliver?

What can you say about God this Christmas season?

As you find the words, share them with others. But
they could be just between you and God. That's okay,
too. Mary's words here lead us to praise God. Jesus
hasn't been born yet, and Mary has a long road
ahead of her. In fact, she has a literally long road
ahead of her to Bethlehem.

In God's wisdom, He would have her travel a long
and bumpy road while nine months pregnant. She
would deliver her baby, our Redeemer, without the
help and support of her mother and father. She
would be in a faraway place with no reservations for
a comfortable bed for herself or her baby.

Mary knew all of this but still praised God, because the promise of Jesus was bigger than her circumstances.

Jesus is the reason for Christmas.

Jesus is worth following God's plan.

Jesus is the Messiah!

Jesus is worth following, even if He's leading down a bumpy road to His birth and there is no extra room at the inn. Perhaps you are on a bumpy path. Follow Jesus. Even if it is a path that God has laid out before you, follow Jesus along the bumpy path.

Mary Knew Jesus is the Redeemer

Jesus is Mary's Redeemer and Jesus is your Redeemer.

You need Jesus.

This is true not just at Christmas time, but for every moment of your life. Mary knew Jesus is the Redeemer. Others knew too. Let's glance at Luke 2.

> When the angels went away from them into heaven, the shepherds said to one another, "Let us go over to Bethlehem and see this thing that has happened,

which the Lord has made known to us."
And they went with haste and found
Mary and Joseph, and the baby lying
in a manger. And when they saw it,
they made known the saying that had
been told them concerning this child.
And all who heard it wondered at what
the shepherds told them. But Mary
treasured up all these things, pondering
them in her heart. (Luke 2:15-19, ESV.)

Mary treasured up all the things that the
shepherds said about Jesus. She already knew,
but the shepherds verified what she knew and
strengthened her belief in her son.

Mary Knew That Jesus Changes Everything

Jesus had already changed Mary's life. Mary knew
who this baby was. Mary knew what the birth of
Jesus would mean for her people. Jesus changes
everything.

Has Jesus changed you?

Jesus can change your life.

Have you let Jesus change you?

If so, how has He changed you? What worship do you need to give to God this Christmas because of this gift of Jesus, redemption, and life change?

Have you let Jesus change you?

If not, why not?

Why would you reject this gift of God's grace? Why would you choose to not allow Jesus to change you? God's plans for you are better for you. Your plans will lead to a mess, a terrible mess.

Whatever messy situation you find yourself in this Christmas, look for God. He is working. He is there. God is with you. "We shall call his name Immanuel," which means God with us. God is with you. Let Jesus change you this Christmas.

Chapter Four

Jesus

For to us a child is born,
to us a son is given;
and the government shall be
upon his shoulder,
and his name shall be called
Wonderful Counselor, Mighty
God,
Everlasting Father, Prince of Peace.
(Isaiah 9:6.)

Three Things About Jesus to Worship This Christmas

1. Jesus was born as a child.

"For to us a child is born,
    to us a son is given;"

J esus, the Son of God, the Creator of the universe, became human. He entered this world the same way you and I did. Jesus was a baby. He grew up as a child, lived through his teenage years, and he was an adult.

Jesus understands what you are going through. He knows what it's like being one of us. He faced temptation. Jesus cried. He loved. Jesus experienced pain and loss. Jesus is worthy of worship this morning because He was born as a child.

2. Jesus is the ruler of everyone and everything.

> "and the government shall be upon his shoulder,"

Jesus is God. Not only did He become human, but Jesus has always existed. He is God. Jesus is fully human and fully divine. It's a tough idea to fully understand, but it is true and it's only true in Jesus.

As God, Jesus rules the lives of those who follow Him. Jesus is the ruler of those who don't follow Him, too. It is far better to follow the ruler than to be in rebellion against Him. Especially since He is a gentle and kind ruler full of love and grace. Jesus as ruler is what it means that Jesus is the Lord. He reigns, He is in charge; He is the boss.

Isaiah says that even governments must submit to His rule. Jesus is worthy of worship because He is the ruler of everyone and everything.

3. Jesus reveals God's character.

As fully God and fully human, Jesus can uniquely reveal God's character to us. You can know more about God as you look at Jesus. You can worship Jesus this Christmas because He reveals God's character to you. Isaiah gives four ways that Jesus reveals God's character.

> "and his name shall be called
> Wonderful Counselor, Mighty
> God,
> Everlasting Father, Prince of Peace."

Jesus is worthy of worship this morning because He reveals God's character to us.

Wonderful Counselor

As Wonderful Counselor, Jesus reveals to us God's wisdom and wonder. If you have ever sat with a counselor, you are seeking input and wisdom as you deal with something that is too much for you to handle, alone. A counselor helps you through a season or a circumstance. God is full of wisdom, and Jesus reveals that wisdom to us. But Jesus is not just any counselor. Jesus is the Wonderful Counselor. The wisdom and counsel you receive from Jesus causes you to be full of wonder and amazement.

As you know Jesus as Wonderful Counselor, you trust Jesus hears you when you seek Him and can lead you in ways you may not understand, but know they are good. God's plans are better than our plans. Follow His plans and His wisdom.

Jesus reveals God's character of wisdom and wonder. Jesus is your Wonderful Counselor.

Mighty God

As Mighty God, Jesus reveals God's strength. Because Jesus is fully God and fully human, He is a child that was born and He is mighty to save. John Owen, a puritan theologian and church leader from the 1600s, says this about Jesus:

> That the same person should be "the mighty God" and a "child born," is neither conceivable nor possible, nor can be done, but by the union of the

divine and human natures in the same person.—John Owen.

Jesus not only understands you, but He can do something about the messy situations you find yourself in. He can rescue you from your sin.

Jesus reveals God's character of strength. Jesus is your Mighty God.

Everlasting Father

As the Everlasting Father, Jesus reveals God's loving and tender care. God created you and loves you. He is good. He has always been good and He will always continue to be good. Your circumstances may change and you may have a limited perception of how God is working, but know that God created you and loves you. He is good.

Jesus reveals this to you in that He died to pay the price for your sin and brokenness. Jesus cares so much for you that He willingly endured the humiliating and painful death of the cross to make you right with God. What Jesus did for you on that cross affects you forever. No one can undo what Jesus did for you. His love and care for you is forever.

Jesus reveals God's character of love and care for you forever. Jesus is our Everlasting Father.

Prince of Peace

As Prince of Peace, Jesus reveals God's desire for you to be made right with Him. God is Holy; you are sinful. If left to yourself, you wouldn't choose God. People prefer their mess over God. God's holiness means unholy people can't be with him. When you put dirt on a clean floor, the floor is no longer clean; it's dirty. That's the way it is with you and God. Apart from Christ, you are at war with God because you can't be near Him. Your sin separates you from God.

But God doesn't want to leave you separated from Him. He sent Jesus at Christmas to bring peace between you and Him. Even though people wouldn't choose peace with God, God chooses you and wants to be near you.

Jesus reveals God's character of wanting you to be made right with Him. Jesus is our Prince of Peace.

Your Response to Jesus this Christmas

Christmas deserves a response. Look at the Shepherds in Luke 2 as we see their response to Jesus at Christmas.

> And in the same region there were shepherds out in the field, keeping

watch over their flock by night. And an
angel of the Lord appeared to them,
and the glory of the Lord shone around
them, and they were filled with great
fear. And the angel said to them, "Fear
not, for behold, I bring you good news of
great joy that will be for all the people.
For unto you is born this day in the city
of David a Savior, who is Christ the Lord.
And this will be a sign for you: you will
find a baby wrapped in swaddling cloths
and lying in a manger." And suddenly
there was with the angel a multitude
of the heavenly host praising God and
saying,

"Glory to God in the highest,
and on earth peace among those with
whom he is pleased!"

When the angels went away from them
into heaven, the shepherds said to one
another, "Let us go over to Bethlehem
and see this thing that has happened,
which the Lord has made known to us."
And they went with haste and found
Mary and Joseph, and the baby lying in
a manger. (Luke 2:8-16, ESV.)

Christmas deserves a response. A gift only becomes meaningful when someone receives it. Maybe this Christmas you realize that you have been unfaithful to God. You have felt weak in your faith. Perhaps this Christmas you feel alone, maybe even apart from God. Maybe you know you haven't yet expressed your faith in Jesus. Perhaps you find yourself weary as you wait on something.

The bitterness in your soul becomes clear as you realize you are broken. You have fears you are so afraid of you won't even speak them to yourself or others. Maybe this Christmas you feel guilty and you are just trying to hide. If you find yourself in one of life's messy situations this Christmas, you are not alone.

Christmas deserves a response. Christ is born for you this Christmas. God chose you, even if no one else ever has. God has chosen you this Christmas.

You are precious to God. In whatever messy situation you find yourself in this Christmas, know that you are precious. God loves you. He has given you His very own Son. God has given you a magnificent gift, but it is meaningless until you receive it.

Will you receive the gift of Jesus this Christmas?

About Author

With a passion for discipleship, Gary writes books and creates resources to help individuals and families know and follow Jesus. He joyfully serves as the Senior Pastor of White Plains Baptist Church in Scottsville, Kentucky. Gary is the founder of Discipleship Studio. Gary earned his Masters of Arts in Biblical and Theological Studies from Knox Theological Seminary in Fort Lauderdale, Florida.

Gary and his wife, Emily, live in Scottsville, Kentucky. They have two daughters, Lily and Ruby. Get more information about Gary at discipleshipstudio.com.

Also By Floyd Gary Pierce

Broken: The Problem of Sin
A Storybook for Little Ones
ISBN: 978-1-965044-03-2

Jonah: It's Not About the Whale
ISBN: 978-1-965044-08-7

Marked by Love: The Call to Love God, the Community, and Other Christians
ISBN: 978-1-965044-00-1

My Big Prayers: The Psalms, Part 1
A Devotional Prayer Journal for Little Ones
ISBN: 978-1-965044-02-5

Available at https://discipleshipstudio.com

www.ingramcontent.com/pod-product-compliance
Lightning Source LLC
Chambersburg PA
CBHW071218120626
46546CB00006B/2619